LYING, FALSEHOODS AND DECEPTIONS

(Genesis 3:1-5)

Written by

Ademola Usuanlele & Christiana Usuanlele

Foreword by

Pastor Abraham Olayioye

Reviewed by

**Pastor Olurotimi Odusote, Joan Imoukhuede &
Iredafenevesho Owolabi**

Other Books from the authors:

The Adventures of Princess Pauline,
Prince Ademola Jnr and their Blue Dragon
(Ademola Usuanlele)
Publisher: Groupe Haus Inc. (Second Edition)

Forgiveness
(Ademola Usuanlele and Christiana Usuanlele)
Publisher: Groupe Haus Inc.

Understanding the Heart of a Giver
(Ademola Usuanlele and Christiana Usuanlele)
Publisher: Groupe Haus Inc.

Dedication

To:

Dr Warren & Mrs. Lois Hathaway (My Canadian Parents)

In Memory of:

Apostle (Dr.) Gordon Erharuyi Osagiede (Father in the Lord, RIP)
Mr. Richard & Mrs. Hannah Usuanlele (Parents, RIP)
Madam Elizabeth Tanimowo Kolade (Grandma, RIP)
Prince Olu Eweka (Brother, RIP)
Mrs. Adunni Enogieru Momoh (Sister, RIP)
Mr. Nosa Usuanlele (Brother, RIP)
Mr. Isaac Omolayo Kolade (Cousin, RIP)
Ms. Margaret "Meg" Oseghe (Sister, RIP)
Mr. Samuel "Brother Sam" Oseghe (Brother, RIP)

Appreciation

To God be all the Glory! I want to use this opportunity to thank God and to thank all of you for your support during the writing of this book; Lying, Falsehoods and Deceptions. Special thanks and appreciation to Apostle Deb'rah Eunice Gordon-Osagiede and Bishop David O Oyedepo for building with the help of the Holy Spirit great commissions from which Christiana and I feed from. I give special thanks to my bosses; Christiana "Titilayo" Usuanlele (my co-author), Pauline Usuanlele and Ademola Usuanlele Jnr for their feedback and supervision and because of whom this book was written. Adebisi Usuanlele, Joyce Usuanlele, Emmy Otoijamun, Rtd Brig-General Adamu & Mrs Doreen Yusuf, Brother Chijioke and Sister Ifeoma Odeluga, Sister Osayi Ogieva, Sister Jennifer Esenwa, Ms. Rosaria Obazee, Dr Raymond Asamoah-Barnieh, Mrs. Bintia Osayimwen, Pastor Omoruyi Usuanlele and Dr Uyilawa Usuanlele thank you to all of you for your suggestions, feedback, support, reviews and/or editing of this book.

Thanks to Bishop Emmanuel & Mrs. Bridget Jatau, Pastor Joseph & Pastor (Mrs) Joanna Odidi, Pastor Daniel & Mrs. Grace Adewumi, Late Mr. Isaac and Mrs. Monisola Kolade, Pastor Clifford Odiai, Pastor Bob Jones, Pastor Sunny Adeniyi, Pastor Milverton Ojegun, Pastor Moses Aghahowa and Pastor Clement Igbinidu and all pastors and members of Winners Chapel International Edmonton & Calgary, Canada and all pastors and members of Spirit and Life Family Bible Church & Godhead Prayer Ministries in Benin City, Edo State, Nigeria for your prayers, spiritual and wise Godly counsel. Pastor Rotimi Odusote, Sister Chinyelu Onuorah, Sister Joan Imoukhuede and Pastor Olayioye Abraham, thanks a million times for your reviews, foreword and publishing and spiritual support. Special thanks to Pastor Solomon Nweke for re-igniting the fire of revival in Winners Chapel International Edmonton, Canada. Special thanks also to Forcible Publications and team for all their great efforts to get this book published in conjunction with Groupe Haus Publishing. The last but not the least important, I thank all members of Usuanlele and Oseghe families and all our in-laws for their love and support.

Thank you! Merci beaucoup!

SPECIAL THANKS

A very special thanks to our Mummy-in-the-Lord; Apostle Deb'rah Eunice Gordon-Osagiede for all her untiring and unfailing love and compassion for all of us her children and her children to be. God bless you Supermom!

PEACE PAGE

Peace
Peace of mind
Peace of the Lord

This page is dedicated to all the people around the world who seek peace, promote peace, keep peace, make peace, and have Peace of the Lord.

Philippians 4:6-7

CONTENTS

FOREWORD

In my foreword, I like to reflect on the subject matter of this life repositioned book from destruction to reconstruction.

The authors tried exploring the two-important points of notes that warranted the subject of lying, falsehoods and deceptions as depicted from, *Gen 3:1-6 (KJV);*

1 Now the serpent was more subtil than any beast of the field which the LORD God had made. And he said unto the woman, Yea, hath God said, Ye shall not eat of every tree of the garden? 2 And the woman said unto the serpent, We may eat of the fruit of the trees of the garden: 3 But of the fruit of the tree which is in the midst of the garden, God hath said, Ye shall not eat of it, neither shall ye touch it, lest ye die. 4 And the serpent said unto the woman, Ye shall not surely die: 5 For God doth know that in the day ye eat thereof, then your eyes shall be opened, and ye shall be as gods, knowing good and evil. 6 And when the woman saw that the tree was good for food, and that it was pleasant to the eyes, and a tree to be desired to make one wise, she took of the fruit thereof, and did eat, and gave also unto her husband with her; and he did eat.

This is the same old strategy that Satan has succeeded in using and the same strategy he transferred into human nature to fulfill his mission on a continuous basis on earth as reflected in the above Bible scripture. The strategy is three in one, that is lies, falsehoods and deceptions. Invariably, this whole component is made to achieve one thing, and that is destruction. While reading this book before publication, I understood Jesus Christ's mission on this earth. I call it God's counter plan on the destruction plans of the devil as it was revealed in
John 10:10-11 (KJV);

10 The thief cometh not, but for to steal, and to kill, and to destroy: I am come that they might have life, and that they might have it more abundantly.

11 I am the good shepherd: the good shepherd giveth his life for the sheep

In my own opinion, the authors tried to help us to understand the game plan and the ways that lead to winning the game. In their efforts, they opened our eyes to the give and take strategic plan of Satan to draw the whole world unto himself, but the scripture justified that whatever he presented can only "seems right" but cannot be right, as advised by the Bible scripture from, **Proverb 14:12 (KJV)**

There is a way which seemeth right unto a man, but the end thereof are the ways of death.

In addition to that, they tried to prepare us to make the right choice base on the revelation of the truth as advised by God in the light of the Biblical scripture from, **Deuteronomy 11:26-28 (KJV):**

26. Behold, I set before you this day a blessing and a curse; 27 A blessing, if ye obey the commandments of the LORD your God, which I command you this day: 28. And a curse, if ye will not obey the commandments of the LORD your God, but turn aside out of the way which I command you this day, to go after other gods, which ye have not known.

Going through all the evidences of lying, falsehoods and deceptions as explained in this book and the antidotes against them in the light of the Biblical scriptural insight of the authors, I am convinced that this book is going to be a great factor in the reconstruction of our world. Therefore, I am recommending this book as a must read to all that are committed to the reconstruction of our broken walls in the world such as walls of education, economy, politics, business and religious.

You shall be blessed with this painstaking, truth revealed, wall mending revelation book on the problematic subject. This is a hardcore truth that the world need to know for true liberty and peace.

Pastor Abraham Olayioye, D.D, CACSW.
President, Christ Model International Ministries, Canada.

Part A

INTRODUCTION AND PREPARATION
Lying, Falsehoods and Deceptions*

**Featured as a bonus chapter in our book: Forgiveness (Matthew 6:12)*

Peace of the Lord to you and your beautiful family. Christiana and I thank God for your decision to read this our book on Lying, Falsehoods and Deceptions. It is our prayer that the Holy Spirit will help you in your quest for understanding Lying, Falsehoods and Deceptions and learning how to stop them if they are issues you are contending with in your life. If you are reading this book to teach and counsel others about the dangers of Lying, Falsehoods and Deceptions, you have a great resource in this book. Just believe that anything you ask our Father in heaven through our Lord and Saviour Jesus Christ will be granted to you Matthew 7:7-8.

Matthew 7:7-8 (NKJV)

Keep Asking, Seeking, Knocking
7 "Ask, and it will be given to you; seek, and you will find; knock, and it will be opened to you. 8 For everyone who asks receives, and he who seeks finds, and to him who knocks it will be opened..."

In our present-day societies, lying has become fashionable and cool amongst the young and the old and amongst Christians and non-Christians. It is an easy excuse to get out of every difficult situation without a thorough understanding of the spiritual implications of these lying, falsehoods and deceptions.

Meaning of Lying, Falsehoods and Deceptions:
Lying, Falsehoods and Deceptions denote actions, statements and/or intents that serve to intentionally mislead or misrepresent information to others with or without malicious connotations. It may or may not be injurious to other affected or unaffected parties.

Lying is a Sin. There is no small or big lie. There is no white lie or black lie or blue lie. A lie is a lie and each of them is a Sin. A Sin is a Sin with the same consequences as any other Sin. It does not matter whether it is lying, murder, unforgiveness, witchcraft or sorcery. They carry the same penalty in the Kingdom of God. James 2:10-13:

James 2:10-13 (NKJV)

10 For whoever shall keep the whole law, and yet stumble in one point, he is guilty of all. 11 For He who said, "Do not commit adultery," also said, "Do not murder." Now if you do not commit adultery, but you do murder, you have become a transgressor of the law. 12 So speak and so do as those who will be judged by the law of liberty. 13 For judgment is without mercy to the one who has shown no mercy. Mercy triumphs over judgment.

In Genesis 3, we see how Man (Adam and Eve) fell because of the lie the serpent told them in the garden of Eden. They were deceived by the cunning devilish serpent. They ended up disobeying God and consequently losing their spiritual covering thereby bringing a curse on every man and woman. Satan is the originator and owner of the spirit of lying, deception and falsehood. Please see an excerpt from Genesis 3 below (read the whole chapter 3 if you can):

Genesis 3:1-5 (NKJV)

The Temptation and Fall of Man
3 Now the serpent was more cunning than any beast of the field which the LORD God had made. And he said to the woman, "Has God indeed said, 'You shall not eat of every tree of the garden'?"
2 And the woman said to the serpent, "We may eat the fruit of the trees of the garden; 3 but of the fruit of the tree which is in the midst of the garden, God has said, 'You shall not eat it, nor shall you touch it, lest you die.'"
4 Then the serpent said to the woman, "You will not surely die. 5 For God knows that in the day you eat of it your eyes will be opened, and you will be like God, knowing good and evil."

Exodus 20:16 and Matthew 22:36-40 below are saying the same thing about lying or bearing false witness. It says we shall not bear false witness or lie against our neighbour. If we love our neighbour as ourselves, we would not be bearing false witness or lying against them. These are the commandments of God which when disobeyed put us in full Sin mode. As we see from above in James 2:10-13, lying makes us guilty of all other commandments and Sin.

Exodus 20:16 (NKJV)

16 "You shall not bear false witness against your neighbor.

Matthew 22:36-40 (NKJV)

36 "Teacher, which is the great commandment in the law?"

37 Jesus said to him, "'You shall love the Lord your God with all your heart, with all your soul, and with all your mind.' 38 This is the first and great commandment. 39 And the second is like it: 'You shall love your neighbor as yourself.' 40 On these two commandments hang all the Law and the Prophets."

In Leviticus 19:11-12 below, God has made His mind clear to us about stealing, dealing falsely and lying to one another and the misuse of His name in any circumstance.

Leviticus 19:11-12 (NKJV)

11 'You shall not steal, nor deal falsely, nor lie to one another. 12 And you shall not swear by My name falsely, nor shall you profane the name of your God: I am the Lord.

God also made his mind clear to us about lying and sinful acts in the book of Revelations 21:8 below;

Revelation 21:8 (NKJV)

8 But the cowardly, unbelieving, abominable, murderers, sexually immoral, sorcerers, idolaters, and all liars shall have their part in the lake which burns with fire and brimstone, which is the second death."

Some of the problems caused by lying, falsehoods and deception include;

Lying Causes Sinful Life and Nature
Lying Causes Lack of Peace of Mind
Lying Causes Lack of Everlasting Joy
Lying Causes Negative Impact on Kingdom Advancement
Lying Causes Lack of Faith

Lying Causes Lack of Love
Lying Causes Lack of Unity
Lying Causes Progression to Witchcraft/Wizardry (Sorcery)
Lying Causes Poor Health
Lying Causes Lack of Prosperity

These problems will be discussed in detail in Part B of this book. As a preamble, Lying, Falsehoods and Deceptions is a very serious issue physically and spiritually. Globally, it is more than an epidemic or a plague. It is a problem that is more than all cancers cases, HIV cases and Ebola virus cases and Malaria cases put together. It causes a lot of physical and spiritual problems. Some of which we will look at in Part B.

Lying, Falsehoods and Deceptions is the root of Sin. It is the first Sin introduced by the devil via the serpent in the Garden of Eden to Eve and eventually Adam.

In this book, we will look at the problems caused by Lying, Falsehoods and Deceptions in Part B. We will conclude in Part C with Truth and Reconciliation to God. There is a bonus chapter on Corruption in Part D.

Also, in this book, we will use the words Lying, Falsehoods and Deceptions together or we will use each of them separately with more emphasis on the word Lying. For generalization, we consider them to mean almost the same thing.

God bless you as you read this book in its entirety in Jesus Christ mighty name. Amen.

Part B

Chapter One:
Lying Causes Sinful Life and Nature

Lying, Falsehoods and Deceptions are a gateway for all other types of Sin to enter our hearts. Lying, Falsehoods and Deceptions are deadly and grievous Sinful acts themselves. Lying brings us into a sinful life and nature by opening our lives to other sinful acts and vices. Every lie we tell, every falsehood we engage in and every deception we carry out open our lives to more Sin than we can even imagine. Lying separates us from God and His love.

The people and the institutions or other parties we lie against that are not properly grounded in the faith of Jesus Christ are killed spiritually by these lies, falsehoods and deceptions. It takes the Grace of God for their spirits to be restored. Lies kill the spirits of others and the liars are dead spiritually. We will see this later in this chapter. People that are spiritually grounded in the faith of Jesus Christ can resist these lies and withstand the devastating effects of being a victim of Lying, Falsehoods and Deceptions.

Let us look at what the Word of God says concerning Lying, Falsehoods and Deceptions as they relate to sinful life and nature.

Colossians 3:9 (NKJV)

9 Do not lie to one another, since you have put off the old man with his deeds,

Colossians 3:9 above said we should not lie to one another since we have put off the old man with his deeds. It means that if we are children of God, we should not be engaging in deeds we used to engage in before we got to know Christ because, we supposed to have dropped off old habits and deeds as soon as we surrendered to Christ.

If we have not dropped off old habits and deeds, we may not be connected to Christ. We need to be surrendered to Christ to drop off or put off deeds or habits of the old man such as Lying, Falsehoods and Deceptions.

Romans 7:18 (NKJV)

18 For I know that in me (that is, in my flesh) nothing good dwells; for to will is present with me, but how to perform what is good I do not find.

In Romans 7:18, Apostle Paul is saying that nothing good dwells in his flesh; he can will good things but his flesh prevents him from performing these good things or deeds. All human flesh is like that too. Our flesh is subject to the control of the devil if we do not surrender our lives to Jesus Christ. If we are in Christ old things are passed away and all things become new. We can suppress all sinful life and nature such as lying, falsehoods and deceptions because there are spurred by the devil through the flesh or body.

Genesis 6:5 (NKJV)

5 Then the Lord saw that the wickedness of man was great in the earth, and that every intent of the thoughts of his heart was only evil continually.

In Genesis 6:5, God saw that the wickedness of man was great in the earth and that the intent of the thoughts of man's heart was only evil continually. This situation still exists today. If a man is a liar, a falsifier and a deceiver, this sinful wickedness and continuous evil intents will be his second nature and lifestyle.

However, if we repent of the sin of lying, falsehoods and deceptions, these constant evil intents of the heart and wickedness can be reversed by the power of the Holy Spirit to ensure that we live sin-free and peaceful lives as Christians.

Jeremiah 17:9 (NKJV)

9 "The heart is deceitful above all things,
And desperately wicked;
Who can know it?

From Jeremiah 17:9, we see how the heart that is not given to Jesus Christ can be completely polluted by desperate wickedness and deceitful above all things. When the Spirit of God or the Holy Spirit is not in a heart, anything goes as far as wickedness, deceptions, lying and falsehoods amongst other sinful acts and nature. To avoid this, turn your hearts over to Jesus Christ and He will give you a new clean heart made of flesh and not of stone.

Matthew 7:21-23 (NKJV)

I Never Knew You

21 "Not everyone who says to Me, 'Lord, Lord,' shall enter the kingdom of heaven, but he who does the will of My Father in heaven. 22 Many will say to Me in that day, 'Lord, Lord, have we not prophesied in Your name, cast out demons in Your name, and done many wonders in Your name?' 23 And then I will declare to them, 'I never knew you; depart from Me, you who practice lawlessness!'

Lying, Falsehoods and Deceptions are lawlessness in the eyes of Jesus Christ. Sinful life and nature are lawlessness which result from Sinful acts like lying. Even if you claim to be a believer of Christ and you perform various acts of signs and wonders in His name and call Jesus Christ Lord, Lord. In the last day, you will not be allowed to enter the kingdom of heaven because Jesus Christ will declare to you, I never knew you; depart from Me, you who practice lawlessness according to Matthew 7:21-23 above.

Romans 1:26-32 (NKJV)

26 For this reason God gave them up to vile passions. For even their women exchanged the natural use for what is against nature. 27 Likewise also the men, leaving the natural use of the woman, burned in their lust for one another, men with men committing what is shameful, and receiving in themselves the penalty of their error which was due.
28 And even as they did not like to retain God in their knowledge, God gave them over to a debased mind, to do those things which are not fitting; 29 being filled with all unrighteousness, sexual immorality, wickedness, covetousness, maliciousness; full of envy, murder, strife, deceit, evil-mindedness; they are whisperers, 30 backbiters, haters of God, violent, proud, boasters, inventors of evil things, disobedient to parents, 31 undiscerning, untrustworthy, unloving, unforgiving, unmerciful; 32 who, knowing the righteous judgment of God, that those who practice such things are deserving of death, not only do the same but also approve of those who practice them.

As we can see above in Romans 1:26-32, these are the Sinful life and nature that God can give up people who engage in Lying, Falsehoods and Deceptions to. They are given up to engage in vile passions, they are given over to debased mind; to do things which are not fitting for the Kingdom of God and for true believers of Jesus Christ. These Sinful acts and nature are engaged in by people who are dead in the spirit and in no time, encounter physical death if repentance is not sought from God through Jesus Christ our Lord quickly.

2 Timothy 3:1-7 (NKJV)

Perilous Times and Perilous Men
3 But know this, that in the last days perilous times will come: 2 For men will be lovers of themselves, lovers of money, boasters, proud, blasphemers, disobedient to parents, unthankful, unholy, 3 unloving, unforgiving, slanderers, without self-control, brutal, despisers of good, 4 traitors, headstrong, haughty, lovers of pleasure rather than lovers of God, 5 having a form of godliness but denying its power. And from such people turn away! 6 For of this sort are those who creep into households and make captives of gullible women loaded down with sins, led away by various lusts, 7 always learning and never able to come to the knowledge of the truth.

2 Timothy 3:1-7 is also talking about Sinful life and nature that men and women are engaging in in these last days. Lying, Falsehoods and Deceptions are activities and actions that bring about these unholy lifestyle and nature. Do not get me wrong, these acts listed above are already here with us and they are taking further hold on the society and this world. It becomes obvious that if the Word of God says it will happen in the last days, can we then conclude without any equivocation that we are in the last days for the benefit of doubters?

Repent from the Sin of Lying, Falsehoods and Deceptions so that you do not put your life; physical and spiritual lives and the lives of others in harms way both spiritually and physically. The wages of Sin is death; both Spiritual and physical death. If you have Sin of Lying, Falsehoods and Deceptions in your life, you cannot make it to heaven.

The Wages of Sin is Death

Romans 6:23 below shows that the wages of Sin is death and that the gift of God to those who shun Sin and live a righteous life is eternal life in Christ Jesus our Lord. Put differently, if we have a lying heart, it is a Sin and the Sin will lead to our death spiritually and physically.

Romans 6:23 (NKJV)

23 For the wages of Sin is death, but the gift of God is eternal life in Christ Jesus our Lord.

The Death is Spiritual and Physical Death

When you are a liar, it deposits Sin in your heart. As soon as your heart becomes Sinful it disconnects your spirit man from God the source of its spiritual sustenance resulting in the death of your spirit man. This is the spiritual death. Once the spirit is dead, the physical body becomes a living dead.

The physical body can die at any time because of all the vices the Sinful heart subjects the physical body to. A dead spirit cannot receive eternal life. The only way the body and spirit man can be rescued is by stopping to engage in Lying, Falsehoods and Deceptions and repenting of all the Sin in your life.

We have established that Lying is a Sin; that the Wages of Sin is Death and that Death is Spiritual which eventually leads to Physical Death. Our prayers ARE NOT answered if there is Sin in our lives. You must repent of all Sin especially lying, falsehoods and deceptions before you can come before Jesus Christ; the only Way to God.

Chapter Two:
Lying Causes Lack of Peace of Mind

As the saying goes: Once you tell a lie, you need ten more lies to cover the lie. Before you know it, you are in an endless cycle of telling lies after lies. For amateur liars, this can be disorienting and disturbing to the mind and spirit even to the body. However, those whose hearts and souls have been completely swallowed or consumed by wickedness and evil, they enjoy and are amused by the shear destruction and havoc caused by their lies. They enjoy it because they are engaged in the bidding of their master the devil.

This creates an environment where the liars are restless and without peace of mind because they need more lies to tell from the devil to keep the evil going and to cover up the previous lies they have told others. Those on the receiving end of these lies will remain restless and lack peace of mind because of the negative effects of lies told by the liars. If you are not born again and you do not have the Holy Spirit in you, Jesus Christ is not your Lord and personal saviour and you do not believe in God, you will forever be on the receiving end of the ruthless and devastating effects of lying, falsehoods and deceptions of the devil, its agents and his children.

Lying, falsehoods and deceptions cause so many problems including your loss of peace of mind. Our aim and ultimate purpose here on earth is to have Peace of the Lord which is far higher (but achievable) than the peace and peace of mind being marketed or touted around.

"There is a great peace for those who obey God. But those who do not obey Him can stumble." Psalm 119:165.

Psalm 119:165 (NKJV)

[165] *Great peace have those who love Your law,*
And nothing causes them to stumble.

According to Psalm 119:165, those who love and obey the law of God including; "You shall not lie or bear false witness against your neighbours", will have great peace and nothing will cause them to stumble. If you obey the law, you will have great peace from God and you will not stumble in your ways. Lying will steal your peace and it will make you to stumble.

Leviticus 6:1-5 (NKJV)

6 And the Lord spoke to Moses, saying: 2 "If a person sins and commits a trespass against the Lord by lying to his neighbor about what was delivered to him for safekeeping, or about a pledge, or about a robbery, or if he has extorted from his neighbor, 3 or if he has found what was lost and lies concerning it, and swears falsely—in any one of these things that a man may do in which he sins: 4 then it shall be, because he has sinned and is guilty, that he shall restore what he has stolen, or the thing which he has extorted, or what was delivered to him for safekeeping, or the lost thing which he found, 5 or all that about which he has sworn falsely. He shall restore its full value, add one-fifth more to it, and give it to whomever it belongs, on the day of his trespass offering.

Leviticus 6:1-5 above shows various lying, falsehoods and deceptions scenarios that can cause lack of peace of mind if the liar or liars do not restore or make restitution for them. If this repentance is not done there will be no peace of mind for the liar or liars. The restoration mentioned here is 120% of the value of the sin and trespass committed by lying, falsehoods and deceptions. This is for quantifiable sin and trespasses.

Job 11:3-5 (NKJV)

3. Should your empty talk make men hold their peace?
And when you mock, should no one rebuke you?
4. For you have said,
'My doctrine is pure,
And I am clean in your eyes.'
5. But oh, that God would speak,
And open His lips against you,

From Job 11:3-5 above, when you engage in empty talk or lies, do you expect people to hold their peace and tolerate such nonsense? When you mock others or try to mock God, do you expect that no one will rebuke or confront you? Even if no one complains or rebuke you, God will because lying, falsehoods and deceptions and mockery are sin in His sight; they disrupt the peace here on earth and in the Heavens. So, watch yourself when you engage in empty talks, lies, falsehoods, deceptions and mockery as they can lead to your peace of mind being compromised.

Philippians 4:6-7 (NKJV)

6 Be anxious for nothing, but in everything by prayer and supplication, with thanksgiving, let your requests be made known to God; 7 and the peace of God, which surpasses all understanding, will guard your hearts and minds through Christ Jesus.

Philippians 4:6-7 state that we should be anxious about nothing and gives a Holy recipe of what we need to do to combat anxiety which lying, falsehoods and deceptions can cause for us to obtain the peace of God which surpasses all understanding. Do not engage in lying, falsehoods and deceptions. If you do, anxiety can result which will ultimately cost you your peace of mind.

Romans 12:18 (CEB)

18 If possible, to the best of your ability, live at peace with all people.

Romans 12:18 is attainable if liars, falsifiers and deceivers are held in check or curtailed. If they are allowed free reign, it will be difficult if not impossible for people to live in peace except God intervene.

Matthew 5:9 (NKJV)

9. Blessed are the peacemakers,
*   For they shall be called sons (and daughters) of God.*

True sons and daughters of God (Matthew 5:9) will always make peace but the children and agents of the devil will be constantly engaging in lying, falsehoods and deceptions to disturb the peace enjoyed by the sons and daughters of God. If the children and agents of the devil are around the peace of the children of the God will always be threatened. God will always make a way for the His children to prevail and live in peace.

Romans 14:17-19 (NKJV)
17 for the kingdom of God is not eating and drinking, but righteousness and peace and joy in the Holy Spirit. 18 For he who serves Christ in these things is acceptable to God and approved by men.

19 Therefore let us pursue the things which make for peace and the things by which one may edify another.

Concluding with Roman 14:17-19, we should not worry too much about eating and drinking because that is not what the kingdom of God is about. Instead, we should put our focus on righteousness, peace and joy in the Holy Spirit. It is important we should rely on these things especially, peace and other things which edify the body of Christ Jesus. Achieving this peace and edification requires working strongly on the issue of lying, falsehoods and deceptions amongst believers and unbelievers.

Chapter Three:
Lying Causes Lack of Everlasting Joy

Everlasting joy is defined as a feeling of great unending pleasure and unending happiness through our Lord and Saviour Jesus Christ. A liar, falsifier and deceiver will never have everlasting joy if they refuse to repent of their sin of lying, falsehoods and deceptions. Liars, falsifier and deceivers are an affront to the everlasting joy of believers because they constantly try to provoke anger, offence and revenge in the hearts of believers. But those who know their God will resist the devil in these liars, falsifiers and deceivers and they will always flee from the believers of Jesus Christ (faithfuls in Christ).

Let us go through the Great Word of God to see some relationships between lying, falsehoods and deceptions and everlasting joy.

Philippians 4:4-5 (NKJV)

4 Rejoice in the Lord always. Again I will say, rejoice!

5 Let your gentleness be known to all men. The Lord is at hand.

Philippians 4:4-5 says that we should rejoice in the Lord always. It emphasizes that we should again rejoice. Part of the ways we can make our gentleness known to men is to show compassion and love of Christ by being truthful and avoiding all forms of sin including lying, falsehoods and deceptions when dealing with every man and woman in this world. It is important for us to avoid lying, falsehoods and deceptions because our Lord is at hand. May God guide and protect us as we let our gentleness known to all men especially in area of truth and honesty to ensure and sustain our everlasting joy in Jesus Christ mighty name. Amen.

Isaiah 61:7 (NKJV)

7 Instead of your shame you shall have double honor,
And instead of confusion they shall rejoice in their portion.
Therefore in their land they shall possess double;
Everlasting joy shall be theirs.

From Isaiah 61:7 above, lying, falsehoods and deceptions can cause shame, confusion and they can deprive us of our everlasting joy. However, the Word of God says we shall have double honour instead of shame, instead of the spirit of confusion at play in our lives, we shall rejoice in our portion, we shall possess double in our land and everlasting joy will be our portion in Jesus Christ mighty name. Amen.

Isaiah 65:14 (NKJV)

14. Behold, My servants shall sing for joy of heart,
But you shall cry for sorrow of heart,
And wail for grief of spirit.

According to Isaiah 65:14 above, those who are servants of God by living without sin especially lying, falsehoods and deceptions shall sing for joy of the heart. People whose hearts are filled with lies, falsehoods and deceptions shall cry for sorrow of the heart and wail for grief of spirit. Beware of what you fill your hearts with because they can compromise your everlasting joy.

Psalm 51:12 (NKJV)

12. Restore to me the joy of Your salvation,
And uphold me by Your generous Spirit.

If we are truthful and honest by avoiding lying, falsehoods and deceptions, God will restore to us the joy of His salvation and He will uphold us all the time by His generous Holy Spirit (Psalm 51:12). Only God can do that if we are truthful and honest.

Ecclesiastes 2:26 (NKJV)

26 For God gives wisdom and knowledge and joy to a man who is good in His sight; but to the sinner He gives the work of gathering and collecting, that he may give to him who is good before God. This also is vanity and grasping for the wind.

If we are good in the sight of God by being truthful and honest and shunning every form of lying, falsehoods and deceptions, God will give us wisdom, knowledge and everlasting joy. But if we are sinners, God will make us labour and gather for the benefit of those who are good before Him (Ecclesiastes 2:26).

Ecclesiastes 11:7-10 (NKJV)

7. Truly the light is s
And it is pleasant for the eyes to behold the sun;
8. But if a man lives many years
And rejoices in them all,
Yet let him remember the days of darkness,
For they will be many.
All that is coming is vanity.
Seek God in Early Life
9. Rejoice, O young man, in your youth,
And let your heart cheer you in the days of your youth;
Walk in the ways of your heart,
And in the sight of your eyes;
But know that for all these
God will bring you into judgment.
10. Therefore remove sorrow from your heart,
And put away evil from your flesh,
For childhood and youth are vanity.

From Ecclesiastes 11:7-10 above, we see a long wise narrative from the Word of God which encourages the youth to "Seek God early in life" to ensure that they get a prolonged everlasting joy because the alternative will lead to a life of vanity and sorrow in their heart and evil in their flesh. The Word of God gives life.

Jeremiah 15:16 (NKJV)

16 Your words were found, and I ate them,
And Your word was to me the joy and rejoicing of my heart;
For I am called by Your name,
O Lord God of hosts.

From Jeremiah 15:16 we see that if we find God's Word like the scriptures we have quoted in this book and many more in the Holy Bible, we should eat them. Eat them means we should read them, commit them to our mind or heart and act on them by faith; believe it is as stated by God without a doubt.

The Word of God we eat allows us to have joy in the Lord and everlasting rejoicing of our heart. A heart filled with lying, falsehoods and deception cannot fully eat and digest the Word of God to have everlasting joy except you forego sin including lying, falsehoods and deceptions.

Isaiah 51:11 (NKJV)

11 So the ransomed of the Lord shall return,
And come to Zion with Singing,
With everlasting joy on their heads.
They shall obtain joy and gladness;
Sorrow and sighing shall flee away.

Taking Isaiah 51:11 in context, we see that lying, falsehoods and deceptions allows the devil to hold us as a ransom because of our sin. Repenting of the sin of lying, falsehoods and deceptions give us the opportunity to return to Zion or house of God or God's Kingdom with singing, with Everlasting joy on our heads. We shall obtain joy and gladness. Sorrow and sighing that comes with lying hearts shall flee away from us.

God designed and made us fully loaded with everlasting joy. Sin such as lying, falsehoods and deceptions shut down that function in us and they even try to shut down that function of everlasting joy in the lives of people we lie against. This lying sin and any other sin for that matter is not taken lightly by God. The punishment on the earth here is topped off with a life in hell for eternity. Save yourself the pain today; give your life to Jesus Christ today so that He will free you from the torture here on earth and eternal torment in hell. Jesus Christ knows how to protect His people. God bless as you choose life with Jesus Christ. Amen.

Chapter Four:
Lying Causes Negative Impact on
Kingdom Advancement

Lying & Kingdom Advancement

A lying heart cannot effectively and spiritually engage in Kingdom Advancement warfare prayers and outreaches to win and retain souls for God's Kingdom. This is because lying is a Sin. A Sinful heart does not belong to the Kingdom of God Since it does not have righteousness.

Meaning of Kingdom Advancement:
This is the deliberate effort of born again Christians to fulfill the Word of God in Matthew 6:33 by engaging in activities like prayer warfare, outreaches, crusades and evangelisms to win and retain souls for the Kingdom of God. When this effort is engaged in and is mixed with faith and righteousness, there is the assurance by God in Matthew 6:33 that all other things we desire shall be added to us.

Below is the Word of God as a setup:

Matthew 6:33 (NKJV)

33 But seek first the kingdom of God and His righteousness, and all these things shall be added to you

Matthew 6:33 is the Word of God that forms the basis for Kingdom Advancement efforts and benefits. Being righteous means we are in right standing with Jesus Christ, we do not harbour the spirit of lying, falsehoods and deceptions in our hearts amongst other things commanded by Jesus Christ.

Nehemiah 1:7 (NKJV)

7 We have acted very corruptly against You, and have not kept the commandments, the statutes, nor the ordinances which You commanded Your servant Moses.

When we lie, falsify and deceive, we are acting corruptly against God, we are breaking the commandments, the statutes and ordinances that God has passed down to us through His servant Moses (Nehemiah 1:7). A corrupt heart cannot be righteous and an unrighteous heart cannot advance the Kingdom of God.

1 Corinthians 10:13 (NKJV)

13 No temptation has overtaken you except such as is common to man; but God is faithful, who will not allow you to be tempted beyond what you are able, but with the temptation will also make the way of escape, that you may be able to bear it.

From 1 Corinthians 10:13, we can see that we cannot be allowed by God to be tempted beyond what we can withstand. If we are believers and we still engage in lying, falsehoods and deceptions, we should check our hearts to determine if we are truly believers of Jesus Christ. As believers if we are unable to engage in Kingdom Advancement activities because of lying, falsehoods and deceptions, we should check our hearts because we ought to be able to overcome this sin of lying, falsehoods and deceptions by the power of God through the Holy Spirit.

Colossians 3:2 (NKJV)

2 Set your mind on things above, not on things on the earth.

To be successful in Kingdom Advancements, we must set our mind on the things above in Heaven and not on the things on earth (Colossians 3:2). Lying, falsehoods and Deceptions prevent us from focusing on the things above because they are sin which disconnect us from the heavenlies.

1 Corinthians 13:1 (NKJV)
The Greatest Gift

13 Though I speak with the tongues of men and of angels, but have not love, I have become sounding brass or a clanging cymbal.

In 1 Corinthians 13:1, Apostle Paul spoke about being all spiritual without love is useless to the Kingdom of God. The same can be said of trying to advance the Kingdom of God with a lying and deceitful heart. The Advancement of the Kingdom of God is powered by love. The Kingdom of God is built by love. Jesus is love and Jesus is the Word of God. God is love.

Lying, Falsehoods and Deceptions kill the love of God in your hearts. If the love of God cannot reside in your hearts, you have created a Kingdom of hatred, anger, resentment amongst other issues in your heart because of Lying, Falsehoods and Deceptions. Remember that lying is a Sin. The wages of Sin is death.

From all we have seen in this chapter, a lying heart is a sinful heart. A sinful heart does not have the love of God. Only a heart filled with the love of God can truly be righteous and only a righteous heart can successfully advance the Kingdom of God. So, if you have a lying heart, please repent and reconcile your heart back to Jesus Christ so that you can truthfully engage in God's Army to advance His Kingdom and receive all the other things that comes with advancing the Kingdom of God (Matthew 6:33). God bless you and your beautiful family in Jesus Christ mighty name. Amen.

Chapter Five:
Lying Causes Lack of Faith

Lying, Falsehoods and Deceptions collectively is a grave sin which form the foundations upon which nearly every other sin are built upon. When you have such foundations in your life, faith in God will be the last thing such a life or such a heart or mind will consider.

Lying, Falsehoods and Deceptions occupy the same spot in your heart where your faith resides. Darkness and Light cannot stay together. If you want the Light of God to come into your heart, you must be ready to get delivered from the Spirit of lying, falsehoods and deceptions and by having faith in the Spirit of God (Spirit of Love).

Let us look at the meaning of faith from the Holy Bible and relate the Word of God concerning how lying, falsehoods and deceptions can cause lack of faith in our lives and lives of our families, friends and neighbours.

Meaning of Faith:

Hebrews 11:1 (NKJV)

11 Now faith is the substance of things hoped for, the evidence of things not seen.

John 5:24 (NKJV)

Life and Judgment Are Through the Son
24 "Most assuredly, I say to you, he who hears My word and believes in Him who sent Me has everlasting life, and shall not come into judgment, but has passed from death into life.

If we hear and believe the Word of God and believe in the God that sent Jesus Christ to us, we will have everlasting life and escape judgment by passing from death into life (John 5:24). Not believing the Word of God and Jesus Christ the Son of God who brought us the Word of God and in fact who is the Word of God, we are living in denial and lying outrightly to ourselves and to those who know and hear us live in this denial of Christ and the Word of God.

Denial of the Word of God is a sin. If we are denial of the Word of God, it shows we have no faith in God, His Word, His Son Jesus Christ and His Holy Spirit. Without faith, it is impossible to know God, to serve God, to please God and to escape the Judgment to pass from death into life. Please see Hebrews 11:6 below.

Hebrews 11:6 (NKJV)

6 But without faith it is impossible to please Him, for he who comes to God must believe that He is, and that He is a rewarder of those who diligently seek Him.

From Hebrews 11:6, it is very clear and understandable that if we do not have faith, we cannot please God and we get no reward from God. Every liar, falsifier and deceiver is a sinner and every sinner does not have faith. The moment you become a liar and by implication a sinner, you cannot please God because you have no faith in Him. Instead you have faith in the devil; who is the master and owner of all sinners. As a lying, faithless sinner, you will miss your reward as a diligent seeker and faithful believer in Jesus Christ.

Romans 10:17 (NKJV)

17 So then faith comes by hearing, and hearing by the word of God.

Hebrews 11:1-3 (NKJV)
By Faith We Understand

11 Now faith is the substance of things hoped for, the evidence of things not seen.

2 For by it the elders obtained a good testimony.

3 By faith we understand that the worlds were framed by the Word of God, so that the things which are seen were not made of things which are visible.

From Romans 10:17 and Hebrews 11:1-3 we see that our faith in God and hope for things we want from God comes **by hearing,** and **hearing by** the Word of God. The first hearing (**by hearing**) here allows us to receive the Word of God by salvation and for growth in the knowledge of God and to 'clean up our act' in terms of repentance, stopping lying, falsehoods and deceptions and to build our hearts and soul up for the next stage of "**hearing by** the Word of God".

This "**hearing by** the Word of God" is often confused by many including Ministers of the Word of God. God has revealed to Ademola that this **hearing** is a state you get to whereby everything you hear, say or do is by the Word of God which you started receiving from the first "**hearing**" and the Word of God you have continued to hear which is faith.

Faith can only be attained if you succeed in crossing the first **hearing** stage by repentance, stopping of all forms of sin including lying, falsehoods, deceptions, forgiveness and building your hearts and souls or minds with the Word of God.

With this faith of God, you can accomplish anything through Christ Jesus. The world and the universe were formed by faith and these things which we see today are all formed from things which we cannot see by the power of God through Jesus Christ.

Matthew 6:25-34 (NKJV)

Do Not Worry

25. "Therefore I say to you, do not worry about your life, what you will eat or what you will drink; nor about your body, what you will put on. Is not life more than food and the body more than clothing?

26. Look at the birds of the air, for they neither sow nor reap nor gather into barns; yet your heavenly Father feeds them. Are you not of more value than they?

27. Which of you by worrying can add one cubit to his stature?

28. "So why do you worry about clothing? Consider the lilies of the field, how they grow: they neither toil nor spin;

29. and yet I say to you that even Solomon in all his glory was not arrayed like one of these.

30. Now if God so clothes the grass of the field, which today is, and tomorrow is thrown into the oven, will He not much more clothe you, O you of little faith?

31. "Therefore do not worry, saying, 'What shall we eat?' or 'What shall we drink?' or 'What shall we wear?'

32. For after all these things the Gentiles seek. For your heavenly Father knows that you need all these things.

33. But seek first the kingdom of God and His righteousness, and all these things shall be added to you.

34. Therefore do not worry about tomorrow, for tomorrow will worry about its own things. Sufficient for the day is its own trouble.

Looking at the Word of God in Matthew 6:25-34, we see Jesus Christ taking His time to get worries out of the mind of His disciples, followers and the other people who were present at this gathering. You may be wondering how does this "Do Not Worry" message relate to lying, falsehoods and deceptions. It goes like this, when we have faith in Jesus Christ, the Holy Spirit and God the Father, we are likely not to engage in lies, falsehoods and deceptions and as a result, we have less to worry about. A lot of lying, falsehoods and deceptions are a result of fears and worries.

Strangely enough, a lot of worries and fears people face the other way around are created from lies, falsehoods and deceptions that they have engaged in before or that they are planning to engage in in the future. It is really a vicious, very vicious cycle of stress and torture by the devil and its agents. The lying, falsehoods and deceptions get to a point where it will include fears and worries of the law and law enforcement agencies. A typical case in point is corruption; which is a hodgepodge of fears, worries, lying, falsehoods, deceptions and stealing and in some cases, physical and sexual violence and murder. Anyone who is involved in this kind of mess or hodgepodge except through repentance cannot have faith in God and cannot please God.

Back to the message of Jesus Christ, when we get into worrying and fears, we lose our faith in God and once our ability to rely on God is gone, we now rely on our own ability and the devil's guidance. The devil's guidance put us in a state of survival including dubious means such as lying, falsehoods, deceptions, worries and fears and the whole hodgepodge mentioned above. Only Jesus Christ can save us from this kind of mess because without faith we cannot please God or receive from God or even rely on God. Think about it, do you want to rely, receive and please God? If you do, check yourself. Are you in a lying hodgepodge or are considering entering one? Do not even dare it. Some people end up in jail for it, some die in the jail and some die from it without even going to jail. Families, peoples and nations are in all kinds of turmoil today because of lying, falsehoods and deceptions and the arising hodgepodges.

To top it off, those who do not repent or get born again before they die or before Jesus Christ returns get to go spend the rest of eternity in blazing hot hell. I pray you get the courage to repent before it is too late. God bless you and your beautifully blessed family in Jesus Christ mighty name. Amen.

Chapter Six:
Lying Causes Lack of Love

Love and lying, falsehoods and Deceptions are they a great mix or a toxic mix? In the worldly relationships, some believe you need to live a life of lies, falsehoods and deception to be loved and to keep love alive and interesting. Lying and love in the real sense are opposites. It is like mixing light with darkness. Light and darkness cannot stay together. If light (true love) appears, darkness (lies, falsehoods and deceptions) disappear. That is the way it should be if Jesus Christ is in the middle of the love because Jesus Christ (God) is love. (See 1 John 4:8,16-19 below) We will look at God's kind of love which he expressed strongly through giving us Jesus Christ His only begotten Son to die for our sake to get us everlasting life. See John 3:16 below.

John 3:16 (NKJV)

16 For God so loved the world that He gave His only begotten Son, that whoever believes in Him should not perish but have everlasting life.

1 John 4:8 (NKJV)

8 He who does not love does not know God, for God is love.

1 John 4:16-19 (NKJV)

16 And we have known and believed the love that God has for us. God is love, and he who abides in love abides in God, and God in him.

The Consummation of Love

17 Love has been perfected among us in this: that we may have boldness in the day of judgment; because as He is, so are we in this world. 18 There is no fear in love; but perfect love casts out fear, because fear involves torment. But he who fears has not been made perfect in love. 19 We love Him because He first loved us.

What is love? How can we recognize love when we see it? Love is the feelings, emotions and affection and desires one person, a group of persons or a group of people have for another person, a group of persons or a group of people. Sometimes, if not most of the time, there is a reason or a group of reasons this love is there. These reasons can even be regarded sometimes as conditions for the love. There are various variations to the use of the word love and various variations to the practices of love among humans both believers of the gospel of Jesus Christ and unbelievers.

We now know from the Word of God (Jesus Christ) through the Holy Bible and through revelations that God through His only begotten Son; Jesus Christ who died for our sake, made a special kind of love available to us. This love trumps all other love because this love is unconditional love. It is called AGAPE LOVE. The love is already there for us even before we were born. We do not work to earn or merit it. It has been provided as Jesus Christ came to the earth, lived, died and rose to Heaven to confirm this unconditional and unmerited love. As part of this love, we have the Holy Spirit to comfort us here in all things on earth and Jesus Christ our Lord and personal Saviour is on the righthand side of our Father God making intercessions on our behalf. How can you beat this kind of love?

To recognize this Agape love, please see 1 Corinthians 13 below to have taste of Agape love. Use it to know what is the type or level of lover you are right now or to see where Jesus wants you to be. It is a long read but it is worth every letter used in writing it. You are blessed and highly favoured in Jesus Christ mighty name. Amen.

1 Corinthians 13 (NKJV)

The Greatest Gift

13 Though I speak with the tongues of men and of angels, but have not love, I have become sounding brass or a clanging cymbal. 2 And though I have the gift of prophecy, and understand all mysteries and all knowledge, and though I have all faith, so that I could remove mountains, but have not love, I am nothing. 3 And though I bestow all my goods to feed the poor, and though I give my body to be burned, but have not love, it profits me nothing.
4 Love suffers long and is kind; love does not envy; love does not parade itself, is not puffed up; 5 does not behave rudely, does not seek its own, is not provoked, thinks no evil; 6 does not rejoice in iniquity, but rejoices in the truth; 7 bears all things, believes all things, hopes all things, endures all things.

8 Love never fails. But whether there are prophecies, they will fail; whether there are tongues, they will cease; whether there is knowledge, it will vanish away. 9 For we know in part and we prophesy in part.10 But when that which is perfect has come, then that which is in part will be done away.

11 When I was a child, I spoke as a child, I understood as a child, I thought as a child; but when I became a man, I put away childish things. 12 For now we see in a mirror, dimly, but then face to face. Now I know in part, but then I shall know just as I also am known.

13 And now abide faith, hope, love, these three; but the greatest of these is love.

Matthew 22:36-40 (NKJV)

36 "Teacher, which is the great commandment in the law?"

37 Jesus said to him, "'You shall love the Lord your God with all your heart, with all your soul, and with all your mind.' 38 This is the first and great commandment. 39 And the second is like it: 'You shall love your neighbor as yourself.' 40 On these two commandments hang all the Law and the Prophets."

In Matthew 22:36-40, Jesus the greatest teacher and the greatest lover told us that the first and second great commandments are about loving God and loving our neighbours. Our "neighbours" here are our immediate and extended families, our friends, our co-workers, our school mates, our business partners, our neighbours, our enemies and anybody we interact with or encounter in our lifetime on this earth. Remember that we can only get and keep this love if we are always truthful and honest with our "neighbours" despite their failings and shortcomings. We must remain righteous too in all our dealings with God and the rest of the Trinity when it comes to all Sin in our lives.

Now, looking at Exodus 20:16 and Leviticus 19:11 below and Matthew 22:36-40 above, we see how God clearly declared in His commandments that we should not lie, bear false witness or be deceitful. It is a sin that should and must be avoided at all cost. The correlation here is that if you lie against anyone, you kill their spirit and mostly kill everything good inside of the person. If there was any love between you the liar and the person you lied against, that love is most of the time converted to useless and damaging energy in the form of hatred, resentment, unforgiveness, vengefulness and a lot of times murder in the heart. It takes only the grace of God and a heart that knows God with the spirit of forgiveness properly located in their heart for the devil not to take charge and rejoice for a new convert to his Kingdom of darkness. Lying, falsehoods and deception is an assault on the heart where love; all love including Agape love resides. True love cannot stand or tolerate lies. If it does, it is not a true love. Both cannot reside in the same heart.

Exodus 20:16 (NKJV)

16 "You shall not bear false witness against your neighbor.

Leviticus 19:11 (NKJV)

11 'You shall not steal, nor deal falsely, nor lie to one another.

The lies are a contaminant, a toxin, a dangerous virus, a vicious cancer which can spread fast, far and wide if not contained quickly by the power of the Holy Ghost. It can jump from human to human and from inanimate objects to human and from humans to inanimate objects. It is that dangerous. In conditions like these, love especially Agape love cannot thrive. Fears, worries, unforgiveness, revenges, violence, unrest, unloveliness, murder, gossips, rumours, more lies, falsehoods and deceptions will be the order of the day amongst the neighbours, people and nations. Loving your neighbours and loving God according to Matthew 22:36-40 cannot be achieved under these sinful conditions.

The only way this chaos can stop is when the Word of God; Jesus Christ; God of love steps in through conviction and conversion of the souls of men, women, boys and girls by their repentance and receiving the spirit of forgiveness and the spirit of love; Agape love.

Watch the liars, the falsifiers and the deceivers, their presence makes it impossible for love to be present. Where there is no love, there is every form of evil works (James 3:16). We are admonished to love and not tell lies and if we do love, whatever we lay our hands to do shall prosper in Jesus Christ mighty name. Amen. Jesus loves you.

Chapter Seven:
Lying Causes Lack of Unity

A true and complete unity cannot be achieved or obtained if lies and liars are involved directly or indirectly in the united purpose or party. This is because lying, falsehoods and deceptions are the first tier or foundation sin upon which most other obvious and non-salient sin are built. If you can identify the liars and restore them and their lives through repentance, conviction and conversion to the state where Jesus Christ wants them to be, it is easy to settle down to uniting for a good and/or godly cause.

Unity means there is a sense of togetherness, there is a sense of cooperation and a sense of comraderies, a sense of common purpose and if there is unity, there is a presence of love depending on the type of relationship between the party or parties in unity. If unity and love are present, it is almost automatic for peace to be present. To top it off, if this is a Christian unity whether in marriage, business, church, school and any form of unity that Christ is professed. The hand of Jesus Christ, the Holy Spirit and God the Father will manifest itself evidentially in all the things concerning the lives of all parties involved in the united effort. The team efforts and performance will be beyond imagination.

There are all kinds of unity touted around. The unity that is based on the Gospel of Christ or the Word of God which is Jesus Christ, will achieve or accomplish great things and the unity which is based on evil or carnally-minded things will only achieve bad or evil things and this kind of unity will really struggle to do good. Even when it seems like there is a good intention or motive, when you look closely with a spiritual eye or even with the physical eye, you will find some mischief or evil no matter what the intention of the united team or party is.

If you look at Genesis 11:1-9 below, it is the story of the Tower of Babel which was being built without any intention to honour or glorify the name of God. The people had one purpose, one language and one speech which made it easy for them to do anything good or bad because there was no barrier or hindrance among them. God was concerned about this power from their unity. He promptly confused their language before they caused too much trouble for Him due to their unity. Please see the excerpt below;

Genesis 11:1-9 (NKJV)

The Tower of Babel

11 Now the whole earth had one language and one speech. 2 And it came to pass, as they journeyed from the east, that they found a plain in the land of Shinar, and they dwelt there. 3 Then they said to one another, "Come, let us make bricks and bake them thoroughly." They had brick for stone, and they had asphalt for mortar. 4 And they said, "Come, let us build ourselves a city, and a tower whose top is in the heavens; let us make a name for ourselves, lest we be scattered abroad over the face of the whole earth."

5 But the LORD came down to see the city and the tower which the sons of men had built. 6 And the LORD said, "Indeed the people are one and they all have one language, and this is what they begin to do; now nothing that they propose to do will be withheld from them.7 Come, let Us go down and there confuse their language, that they may not understand one another's speech." 8 So the LORD scattered them abroad from there over the face of all the earth, and they ceased building the city.9 Therefore its name is called Babel, because there the LORD confused the language of all the earth; and from there the LORD scattered them abroad over the face of all the earth.

The Psalmist in Psalm 133 below describes how good and how pleasant it is for children of God to dwell together in unity. The Psalmist also describes unity like the precious anointing oil upon the head (v.2). Unity among the children of God gives life forevermore (v.3). This kind of unity that results in life forevermore is only possible if we have hearts that reject every form of lying, falsehoods, deceptions and free ourselves from every form of entanglements of sin in our life.

Psalms 133 (NKJV)

Blessed Unity of the People of God

133 Behold, how good and how pleasant it is
For brethren to dwell together in unity!
2 It is like the precious oil upon the head,
Running down on the beard,
The beard of Aaron,
Running down on the edge of his garments.
3 It is like the dew of Hermon,
Descending upon the mountains of Zion;
For there the Lord commanded the blessing—

Life forevermore.

We have seen from above how sweet unity can be especially if it is mixed with faith and the love of God. However, lying, falsehoods and deception is a toxin, a pollutant and an irritant to unity, peace and love. The presence of falsehoods, lies and deceptions work against the unity of a purpose, the unity of a marriage, the unity of a party, the unity of a Church, the unity of a nation, the unity of a people and even the unity that God or Jesus Christ has purposed for us. Where there is unity, the presence of lying, falsehoods and deceptions creates a lot of misunderstandings and can become a breeding ground for sin infestations thereby leading to disunity. Once there is a sin infestation, every thought or effort at unity will be defeated.

Mark 3:25 (NKJV)

25 And if a house is divided against itself, that house cannot stand.

From Mark 3:25 above, we see that divided or different minds usually stem from lying, falsehoods and deceptions which bring about disunity and eventually break up in churches, marriages, friendship and various kinds of human relationships and interactions.

Philippians 2:1-3 (NKJV)

Unity Through Humility
2 Therefore if there is any consolation in Christ, if any comfort of love, if any fellowship of the Spirit, if any affection and mercy,
2 fulfill my joy by being like-minded, having the same love, being of one accord, of one mind. 3 Let nothing be done through selfish ambition or conceit, but in lowliness of mind let each esteem others better than himself.

Philippians 2:1-3 is very powerful in laying out what Jesus Christ expects from us by being united through humility. We must free our hearts by shunning every form of lying, falsehoods and deceptions. We must shun selfishness, be like-minded and in lowliness of mind let us esteem others above ourselves. Please read and meditate on this scripture above (Philippians 2:1-3). It sums up how to achieve unity. But free up your hearts by shunning lies, falsification and deceits always.

Just like the trinity of God the Father, God the Son and God the Holy Spirit are united in one body. God also created our body to be united in body, soul and spirit. Our body has members that also needs to be united to function as designed by God.

Lying, falsehoods and deceptions which is a Sin creates a disruption in the spirit, soul and body resulting in the Spirit of God departing the Sin-laden heart of the liar.

Lying, falsehoods, deceptions and pride go together in ensuring that the devil uses them against the spirit of unity in marriages, families, Churches and friends. The devil uses lies to cause strife amongst peoples and nations of the world.

Please do not allow the devil to use you for his evil machinations against others. So, repent from all sin of lying, falsehoods and deceptions and continue to refill your heart with the Spirit of God. A family or a people that is united will experience peace, love and joy and God will always command His blessings upon such a family and people. May God help us to be unifiers and not dividers in Jesus Christ mighty name. Amen.

Merci beaucoup! (Thank you!)

Chapter Eight:
Lying Causes Progression to Witchcraft/Wizardry (Sorcery)

Witchcraft/Wizardry (Sorcery) is an advanced or viral sin condition where the complete body, soul and spirit of man or woman have been completely yielded or submitted to the enemy of God; lucifer for both clandestine and daylight utilization in both flesh and spirit. The use that lucifer puts its people to are unimaginable evil and crime. Some are sickening and others are pure spooky, scary and shocking.

The control lucifer has over the witches and wizards allow them to proffer or conjure up more atrocious evil and crime for their master lucifer. Demons and demonic activities and control and use of evil spirits become a walk in the park for them thereby making them to engage in sorcery, witchcraft and wizardry.

Lying, falsehoods and deceptions as sin channel can, if not checked, progress to witchcraft/wizardry because each sin type has the genetic and spiritual make up of every other sin you can imagine. Each sin is like a seed. If you allow the seed to germinate and grow, it will bring forth and manifest every other sin at any given opportunity. The goal therefore, is to repent as quickly as possible if you have sin because if it germinates and grows or go viral within you, you are in for a real long spiritual battle. Avoid sin at all cost. Repent of your sin as quickly as possible using the power of the Holy Spirit through Jesus Christ.

Lying, Falsehoods and Deceptions feed witchcraft, wizardry and sorcery. Witchcraft, wizardry and sorcery feed Lying, Falsehoods and Deceptions. Sin feeds on itself and its hosts. As mentioned earlier, lying is a Sin. There is no small or big lie. There is no white lie or black lie or blue lie. A lie is a lie and each of them is a Sin. A Sin is a Sin with the same consequences as any other Sin. It does not matter whether it is lying, murder, unforgiveness, witchcraft or sorcery. They carry the same penalty in the Kingdom of God. James 2:10-13:

James 2:10-13 (NKJV)

10 For whoever shall keep the whole law, and yet stumble in one point, he is guilty of all. 11 For He who said, "Do not commit adultery," also said, "Do not murder." Now if you do not commit adultery, but you do murder, you have become a trans-

gressor of the law. *12 So speak and so do as those who will be judged by the law of liberty. 13 For judgment is without mercy to the one who has shown no mercy. Mercy triumphs over judgment.*

Sin such as lying, falsehoods and deceptions make the flesh to work against the spirit of God resulting in works of the flesh Galatians 5:16-21.

Galatians 5:16-21 (NKJV)

Walking in the Spirit

16 I say then: Walk in the Spirit, and you shall not fulfill the lust of the flesh. 17 For the flesh lusts against the Spirit, and the Spirit against the flesh; and these are contrary to one another, so that you do not do the things that you wish. 18 But if you are led by the Spirit, you are not under the law.
19 Now the works of the flesh are evident, which are: adultery, fornication, uncleanness, lewdness, 20 idolatry, sorcery, hatred, contentions, jealousies, outbursts of wrath, selfish ambitions, dissensions, heresies, 21 envy, murders, drunkenness, revelries, and the like; of which I tell you beforehand, just as I also told you in time past, that those who practice such things will not inherit the kingdom of God.

As we can see above in Galatians 5:16-21, Sin of lying, falsehoods and deceptions will make the flesh to work against the Spirit of God thereby resulting in several works of the flesh including sorcery which is witchcraft and wizardry. But if you repent and stop lying and the love of God is in your heart, you will operate in the fruits of the Spirit Galatians 5:22-26 NKJV as listed below.

Galatians 5:22-26 (NKJV)

22 But the fruit of the Spirit is love, joy, peace, longsuffering, kindness, goodness, faithfulness, 23 gentleness, self-control. Against such there is no law. 24 And those who are Christ's have crucified the flesh with its passions and desires. 25 If we live in the Spirit, let us also walk in the Spirit. 26 Let us not become conceited, provoking one another, envying one another.

Deuteronomy 18:10-11 (NKJV)

10 There shall not be found among you anyone who makes his son or his daughter pass through the fire, or one who practices witchcraft, or a soothsayer, or one who interprets omens, or a sorcerer, 11 or one who conjures spells, or a medium, or a spiritist, or one who calls up the dead.

From Deuteronomy 18:10-11 above, God is making clear that none of us should be found making ourselves or our precious children to go through fire or any form of witchcraft, wizardry or sorcery by any means and by any form. Please read again Deuteronomy 18:10-11. If you believe in Jesus Christ, the Holy Spirit and God the Father, stop the lying of any type or form. It leads to other sin which includes witchcraft, wizardry and sorcery. Find godly and biblical ways to impact the Holy Spirit into yourselves and your children to give them a great shot at a life without the troubles, aches and pains that sin will bring to your lives.

Isaiah 30:9 (NKJV)

9 That this is a rebellious people,
Lying children,
Children who will not hear the law of the Lord;

Looking at Isaiah 30:9, the Spirit of God is saying that children; in fact, anyone because we are all children of God, who lies and is rebellious will not hear the law or the Word of God. Children or people who do not hear the Word of God can do or become anything including witches, wizards and sorcerers because the seed of the evil one is firmly planted in their hearts. Only God through Jesus Christ can save them now by repentance and accepting Jesus Christ as their Lord and personal Saviour.

James 3:15 (NKJV)

15 This wisdom does not descend from above, but is earthly, sensual, demonic.

The wisdom being described in the James 3:15 above, is the wisdom behind all sin such as lying, falsehoods, deceptions, witchcraft, wizardry, sorcery amongst others that does not come from God in Heaven instead, they come from the ruler of this earth; the disgraced and fallen angel lucifer who use his demonic powers and influence to seduce the senses of the weak and vulnerable people of this world and enrich his loyal servants and agents.

Please note that if you have or you are using his wisdom, it leads only to one place; life in the lake of fire for eternity. Choose Jesus today so that you can receive the wisdom of God which will take you to eternal joy and peace in Heaven. You will even enjoy the Heaven on earth as we do now waiting for the glorious reunion with Jesus Christ in Heaven. Hallelujah!!!!

Please do not use your heart to fabricate lies against anyone, falsify against anyone and deceive anyone thereby destroying their hearts, lives and even causing deaths of innocent and sometimes vulnerable people. The devil will take advantage of you by introducing evil ideas and plots within your hearts for the people you fabricate lies against in your hearts. The brewing of these plots and ideas can turn you, yes turn you into a witch or wizard for devil's kingdom of darkness. You may not be able to control how far the devil can take you with a lying heart.

Stop, lying, falsehoods and deceptions so that you leave no room for the devil. I pray in Jesus Christ mighty name that you do not allow the devil to make you a witch or wizard today or forevermore. Amen. Jesus loves you more than words can say. Amen

Chapter Nine:
Lying Causes Poor Health

Lying, falsehoods and deceptions is sin that will cause a lot of Spiritual, physical, mental and emotional problems for both the liars and for people who are on the receiving end of these lies, falsehoods and deceptions. Especially if they are not fully grounded in the workings and principles of the kingdom of God. Many of these problems because of the lies can lead to a long list of health challenges that are caused by anxieties, fears and worries that in turn result from lie-telling, falsehoods and deceptions.

There is the constant fear of being caught or exposed for the fast-rising list of lies, falsehoods and deceptions that are required to cover up previously told lies. The liars are burdened by their own lies and tormented by their own master the devil with fears, worries and anxiety. It gets to a point where there are physical manifestations of these burdens of lies, falsehoods and deceptions in the forms of health challenges many of which are not curable with medications and conventional medicine.

The victims of these lies, falsehoods and deceptions can get into bad health conditions if they retain these lies in their body, soul and spirit especially through unforgiveness and lack of faith in God. The only known and proven cure for these medical conditions and for long life in these circumstances, is by repenting and moving close to Jesus Christ who is the author and finisher of our faith and life.

Also, when we serve the Lord our God in every way possible with our time, energy and resources including financial resources, Jesus Christ will take away all our pains resulting from lying and other sinful acts or actions whether we are at the receiving end or the giving end of these various forms of sin that result in poor health in our lives.

SERVING GOD WILL TAKE AWAY SICKNESSES. I am a living witness to the fact that serving God takes away sicknesses. You too can be a living witness and it is free! Please see Exodus 23:25 below to get more insight from the Word of God.

Exodus 23:25 (NKJV)

25 "So you shall serve the Lord your God, and He will bless your bread and your water. And I will take sickness away from the midst of you.

3 John 2 (NKJV)

2 Beloved, I pray that you may prosper in all things and be in health, just as your soul prospers.

3 John 2 is a prayer that we prosper in all things and be in health, just as our souls prosper. A soul or heart filled with lies, falsehoods and deceptions will neither prosper nor be in health. Our body is the temple of the Holy Spirit. Our Spirit is troubled by lies, falsehoods and deceptions.

A troubled Spirit will result to physical, emotional, mental and spiritual stress. Stress leads to a lot of health and spiritual problems which can be avoided or healed by repentance.

Proverbs 17:22 tells us that if we are merry in our hearts, the merriness will be good like medicine to our hearts, body and spirit. But if we allow lying, falsehoods and deceptions or other sin into our hearts/lives, it will break our spirit which will dry our bones.

Proverbs 17:22 (NKJV)
22 A merry heart does good, like medicine,
But a broken spirit dries the bones.

Lying, falsehoods and deceptions and all types of Sin attract all kinds of health-related problems which repentance can heal by the power of the Holy Spirit through Jesus Christ our Lord. Jesus Christ has the power to heal every health condition provided we are willing to forgive all the people that have lied against us and repent of all our Sin if we are on the receiving end of lies, falsehoods and deceptions. On the other hand, if we are the falsifier, liar and deceiver, we must stop all of it and ask Jesus Christ for forgiveness and repent with total commitment to God through Jesus Christ.

God knows His people and His people know their God. God cannot be mocked. Hence, to benefit from the good and divine health benefit of God, we must be among God's people or children by repenting fully and being totally committed to God. Only Jesus Christ can make this happen. Do you know Jesus Christ? Do you want to know Him as your Lord and personal Saviour? Ask us how to know Jesus Christ.

Chapter Ten:
Lying Causes Lack of Prosperity

A lot of unbelievers believe with full conviction that you can lie, falsify and deceive your way to riches. Many believe that without adding lies, falsehoods and deceptions, it is not possible to get rich or prosper. There is a great distinction between being rich and being prosperous. Being rich simply means you have access or own lots of money, cars, houses and some liquid and non-liquid assets and/or investments. This definition of being rich ends there without taking a holistic view of other factors of life like health, family, peace, salvation, charity and other givings, love of God and Jesus Christ just to name a few.

For prosperity, it is a lot more than being rich. It is a higher level that can only be attained spiritually from God and sustained by God through Jesus Christ our Lord and personal Saviour.

What exactly is prosperity and how is it different from simply being rich. The meaning of Prosperity:

Prosperity is the spiritual state at which by the Power and Spirit of God, everything in our lives is under the control of God through Christ Jesus. Everything includes faith in God, peace of mind, overall health, overall wealth, everlasting joy, love for God and love for your neighbours amongst others. Above all prosperity is having the Spirit of contentment in all things and in all situations.

When you are prosperous, you achieve and accomplish things with so much ease that it will be like magic to onlookers or unbelievers without their knowing that you are operating under a different law or principle from that of the world. Scriptures like Luke 6:38, Philippians 4:13,19 amongst others will power your systems and processes to further increase your wealth. The devourers will be far from your household and stay out of your affairs (Malachi 3:8-11).

From above in this conversation, you can tell that there is a huge difference between getting rich and getting prosperous. If you are a liar, a falsifier and a deceiver, you may get rich; even very rich but you can never be prosperous. No matter how hard you try because prosperity can only come from knowing, believing and serving God through Jesus Christ. If Jesus Christ is not involved, you can be rich but you will never be prosperous. It is the Holy Spirit that gives the power to obtain and keep wealth (Deuteronomy 8:18).

Wealth or riches obtained through lying, falsehoods and deception cannot be sustained for too long. Even if it is sustained in the life time of the acquirer of the unholy wealth, if he or she does not repent before death, he/she will go straight to hell to live there for eternity. After the death of the acquirer of the riches, his/her dependants or estate are most likely going to squander the riches. The bottom line of these facts is that lying, falsehoods and deception will take you to hell, whether you are rich or not. Anyone hell bound will not be allowed to be prosperous or got to heaven.

3 John 2 (NKJV)

2 Beloved, I pray that you may prosper in all things and be in health, just as your soul prospers.

In 3 John 2 we see that it is God's desire and plan for us to be prosperous in all things and be in (great and divine) health, just as our souls prosper. To achieve God's kind of prosperity our souls need to prosper first and our prosperous soul through Jesus Christ will then prosper us in all things. It is just like Matthew 6:33 We seek first the Kingdom of God with our souls and God's righteousness, and God adds all these things in life that make us prosperous including divine health.

Matthew 6:33 New King James Version (NKJV)

33 But seek first the kingdom of God and His righteousness, and all these things shall be added to you

Job 36:11-12 New King James Version (NKJV)

11 If they obey and serve Him,
They shall spend their days in prosperity,
And their years in pleasures.
12 But if they do not obey,
They shall perish by the sword,
And they shall die without knowledge.

In Job 36:11 we have a similar promise from God; if we obey and serve Him (Jesus Christ; see Matthew 6:33 and 3 John 2) in TRUTH and in SPIRIT, we shall spend our days in prosperity and our years in pleasures. But if we do not serve and obey Jesus Christ in TRUTH and in SPIRIT, we shall face the consequences as stated above in Job 36:12.

Psalm 1:1-6 New King James Version (NKJV)

The Way of the Righteous and the End of the Ungodly
1 Blessed is the man
Who walks not in the counsel of the ungodly,
*   Nor stands in the path of sinners,*
*   Nor sits in the seat of the scornful;*
2 But his delight is in the law of the Lord,
*   And in His law he meditates day and night.*
3 He shall be like a tree
*   Planted by the rivers of water,*
*   That brings forth its fruit in its season,*
*   Whose leaf also shall not wither;*
And whatever he does shall prosper.
4 The ungodly are not so,
But are like the chaff which the wind drives away.
5 Therefore the ungodly shall not stand in the judgment,
Nor sinners in the congregation of the righteous.
6 For the Lord knows the way of the righteous,
But the way of the ungodly shall perish.

Psalm 1:1-6 above shows the characteristics of the ungodly (liars, falsifiers and deceivers) and their end thereof and these characteristics of the ungodly are compared side by side with the characteristics of the righteous. It shows how righteousness leads to prosperity amongst other benefits. Whereas, the ungodly "are like the chaff which the wind drives away" (vs 4). The "sinners cannot be in the congregation of the righteous" (vs 5). "But the way of the ungodly (sinners) shall perish" (vs 6).

If you are a liar, a falsifier and a deceiver, you are at a dead end. The outcome of your life is perishing; in most cases physically and spiritually perishing. Become righteous today. Stop all the lies, falsehoods and deceptions today and surrender to Jesus Christ now. Only Jesus Christ the Righteous One can make you righteous. He is waiting for you now. This is the best time to do it before it is too late for you.

If you have the spirit of lying in your heart/soul, you are harbouring Sin in your soul. A soul that is harbouring spirit of lying or other Sin will not prosper and will not be in good Health. A lying heart or soul cannot obey and serve God. Lying hearts or souls cannot spend their days in prosperity and their years in pleasures.

Please stop all kinds of lying, falsehoods and deception without exceptions and see how God will prosper your soul and prosper you in all areas of your life. Suddenly, you will begin to see the dramatical manifestations of prosperity and good health and peace of mind that Jesus Christ promised every true believer of His. Jesus loves you more than words can say.

Part C

Truth and Reconciliation to God

To overcome the spirit of lying, falsehood, deception and other sin, you must re-dedicate your life back to God as a Christian. If you are not a Christian or you are not born again, there is the need for you to be reconciled back to God through our Lord and Saviour Jesus Christ; the only true way to God our Father who is in Heaven.

Looking at John 14:6 below, the Word of God says Jesus Christ is the way, the truth and the life. If we give our lives to Jesus Christ, He will give us His own perfect life and take over our own lives. He will give us the truth instead of the lies that the devil is selling to us at a premium and He will take us on a path that leads to eternal life with our Father God who is in Heaven. There is no other way to get these except through Jesus Christ. Even if you are the smoothest talking liar, demon or devil.

John 14:6 (NKJV)

6 Jesus said to him, "I am the way, the truth, and the life. No one comes to the Father except through Me.

Spiritually and physically, lying, falsehoods and deceptions according John 8:31-32 below, keeps us in physical and spiritual bondage which prevents the ability of liars to enjoy to the fullest the freedom which the Word of God gives to all those who believe in Jesus Christ. This same Word frees every sinner who is involved in lying, falsehoods, deceptions and other sin. Knowing the Word exposes the truth and knowing the truth gives every believer freedom and peace of the Lord.

John 8:31-32 (NKJV)

The Truth Shall Make You Free
31 Then Jesus said to those Jews who believed Him, "If you abide in My word, you are My disciples indeed. 32 And you shall know the truth, and the truth shall make you free."

To protect us from the spirit of lying, falsehoods and deceptions, we are to sanctify ourselves continuously with the truth and this truth is the Word of God. Spend time dissecting and eating the undiluted Word of God which is Jesus Christ. If you have and know the truth, the spirit of lying, falsehoods and deceptions will flee from you and stay far away from your life. See John 17:17 below.

John 17:17 (NKJV)

17 Sanctify them by Your truth. Your word is truth.

Colossians 3:1-17 (NKJV)

Not Carnality but Christ
3 If then you were raised with Christ, seek those things which are above, where Christ is, sitting at the right hand of God. 2 Set your mind on things above, not on things on the earth. *3 For you died, and your life is hidden with Christ in God. 4 When Christ who is our life appears, then you also will appear with Him in glory.*

5 Therefore put to death your members which are on the earth: fornication, uncleanness, passion, evil desire, and covetousness, which is idolatry. 6 Because of these things the wrath of God is coming upon the sons of disobedience, 7 in which you yourselves once walked when you lived in them.

*8 But now you yourselves are to put off all these: anger, wrath, malice, blasphemy, filthy language out of your mouth. 9 **Do not lie to one another**, since you have put off the old man with his deeds, 10 and have put on the new man who is renewed in knowledge according to the image of Him who created him, 11 where there is neither Greek nor Jew, circumcised nor uncircumcised, barbarian, Scythian, slave nor free, but Christ is all and in all.*

Character of the New Man
*12 Therefore, as the elect of God, holy and beloved, put on tender mercies, kindness, humility, meekness, longsuffering; 13 bearing with one another, and forgiving one another, if anyone has a complaint against another; even as Christ forgave you, so you also must do. 14 But **above all these things put on love, which is the bond of perfection.** 15 And **let the peace of God rule in your hearts,** to which also you were called in one body; and be thankful. 16 **Let the word of Christ dwell in you richly** in all wisdom, teaching and admonishing one another in psalms and hymns and spiritual songs, singing with grace in your hearts to the Lord. 17 And whatever you do in word or deed, do all in the name of the Lord Jesus, giving thanks to God the Father through Him.*

From this long Word of scriptures from Colossians 3:1-17, we are being admonished to seek those things which are above and not the earthly things. If we are in Christ, we should do things the way Christ will do them because as believers with Christ in us, we are not expected to engage in worldly carnality like lying, falsehoods and deceptions. These are works of the flesh or carnal mind.

As a New Man (or Woman), we should exhibit qualities and traits of the new Spirit of Jesus Christ that is now resident within us. Above all these qualities and traits, we should put on love, which is the bond of perfection, we should let the peace of God rule in our hearts and lastly, we should let the Word of Christ dwell richly in us. Please take time to read through the entire Colossians 3:1-17 because it will take several pages to go deeper in the message this passage of scriptures is talking about. God bless you real good.

Ephesians 6:14-18 (NKJV)

14 Stand therefore, having girded your waist with truth, having put on the breastplate of righteousness, 15 and having shod your feet with the preparation of the gospel of peace; 16 above all, taking the shield of faith with which you will be able to quench all the fiery darts of the wicked one. 17 And take the helmet of salvation, and the sword of the Spirit, which is the word of God; 18 praying always with all prayer and supplication in the Spirit, being watchful to this end with all perseverance and supplication for all the saints—

Ephesians 6:14-18 above, gives us the way we protect ourselves if we truly want to engage the enemy of God; lucifer and its agents and demons. There is a role for these in every area of practice in our advancement of the kingdom of God spiritually and physically. Our focus here without trying to diminish the importance of others, is the girding our waist with truth. The waist is a very important area of our body, it connects our upper body to our lower body, it also helps to reduce the weight of the upper body on the lower body (legs) and it contains the joints that allow the ease of movement of our body.

In the physical battles, the waist plays a big role in determining if we will succeed or fail in battles. Spiritually to have such functions as the waist does, it is enhanced by being truthful in all things. If you are a liar, a falsifier and a deceiver, spiritually, your waist is exposed and vulnerable and you will be taken down in the battle even before it starts.

The caution here is that we should not, I repeat, we should not bother to engage in any spiritual battle if we know for a fact that we do not have the Spirit of Truth (Jesus Christ) girded on our waist. If you do, you are making yourself available as a free breakfast or lunch to the devil and its agents and demons. I pray at this moment that if you have not received the Spirit of Truth, to receive it now in Jesus Christ mighty name. Amen. Remember that you must be born again to receive this Spirit of Truth (Jesus Christ). God bless you mightily in Jesus Christ name. Amen.

Two Yoruba (a tribe in Western Nigeria in West Africa) adages state:

Ọmọ tó ba paró á pa ènìyàn

English translation:

A child that tells lies will commit murder

Ọmọ tó ba paró á jalè

English translation:

A child that tells lies will steal.

(Yoruba language translations and accents courtesy of Pastor Rotimi Odusote).

An Edo (a tribe in Midwestern Nigeria in West Africa) adage states:

Ọmọ́ ghàá tà òhóghè, ọ́ vbè ghá rhàá, ọ́ vbè ghá ghẹ̀ẹ́

English translation:

A child that tells lies will steal and will prostitute (fornicate and commit adultery).

(Edo language translation and accents courtesy of Pa Gabriel Obazee and Dr Uy-ilawa Usuanlele).

An Ibo (a tribe in Eastern Nigeria in West Africa) adage states:

Onye na asi asi gezu kwa oshi

English translation:

Anybody who lies will also steal.

(Ibo language translation courtesy of Brother Chijioke Odeluga)

What these African adages are saying is that watch liars. They are on a very slippery slope in the pool of Sin. They will end up in other Sinful and criminal activities if they do not repent of the Sin of lying very quickly. Severe damages are being wrought by their lies, falsehoods and deceptions.

Lies, falsehoods and deceptions are a symptomatic expression of a heart filled with Sin and evil which requires deliverance before it spreads like a cancerous tumour. The worst part is that it can be contagious for those who are not on their spiritual guard.

If you know that you have a lying problem; no matter how small you think it may be, ask Jesus Christ to help you get delivered from it before it spreads into other Sinful acts. May God give you the courage to admit that there is a problem and the wisdom to get help. Talk to your pastor in your local church to guide you in the deliverance process. As I saw in an image on Facebook or WhatsApp a few months ago, it says:

"I would rather please God and have a few people upset with me than to please people and have God upset with me" --Author Unknown

We love you for taking the time to read and apply these materials to your Christian life. Thank you and God bless you. See you soon or in Heaven.

Christiana Usuanlele and Ademola Usuanlele.

Part D (Bonus)

Corruption

Corruption is a term that covers a lot of sinful actions and inactions which are meant or carried out or not carried out to prevent things or situation from taking its normal course whether favourable or unfavourable to some or all the parties involved or affected by the actions or inactions.

Let us be clear about this. Corruption is a sin and the wages of sin is death; physical and/or spiritual death. At the end of the day only lucifer and its agents benefit from corruption. But if anyone who is corrupt abandons his/her corruption and all other sin he/she is engaged in to repent and follow Jesus Christ, he/she will be saved by Jesus Christ.

Corruption is a hate child of the devil and a sinful heart with lying, falsehoods and deception providing the DNA for corruption to be birthed and to grow. Even though the Holy Spirit had set the stage for a book on corruption since last year (September/October 2016), during the delivery of chapter five of this book which is on lying causes lack of faith, the Holy Spirit brought the issue of corruption back to the fore as can be seen from the excerpt below from Chapter Five: Lying causes lack of Faith:

"when we have faith in Jesus Christ, the Holy Spirit and God the Father, we are likely not to engage in lies, falsehoods and deceptions and as a result, we have less to worry about. A lot of lying, falsehoods and deceptions are a result of fears and worries.

Strangely enough, a lot of worries and fears people face the other way around, are created from lies, falsehoods and deceptions that they have engaged in before or that they are planning to engage in in the future. It is really a vicious, very vicious cycle of stress and torture by the devil and its agents. The lying, falsehoods and deceptions get to a point where it will include fears and worries of the law and law enforcement agencies. A typical case in point is corruption; which is a hodgepodge of fears, worries, lying, falsehoods, deceptions and stealing and in some cases, physical and sexual violence and murder. Anyone who is involved in this kind of mess or hodgepodge except through repentance cannot have faith in God and cannot please God."

That said, this part D (Bonus), is just a teaser to give you a fore-taste of a more elaborate book on Corruption as God sees it according to the Word of God. In order not to keep you too thirsty, we will just take a sneak peak into it to add to what is already written above in this section.

Genesis 6:11-12 (NKJV)

11 The earth also was corrupt before God, and the earth was filled with violence. 12 So God looked upon the earth, and indeed it was corrupt; for all flesh had corrupted their way on the earth.

Genesis 6:11-12 shows how corrupt the world has become for God and as we alluded in the excerpt, corruption does result in physical and sexual violence even murder/death. Lying, falsehoods and deceptions play a big role in birthing and growing corruption. To rout corruption, every seedling of lies, falsifications and deceptive practices need to be nipped in the bud. This nipping should be done with the Word of God through Jesus Christ our Lord and Saviour.

Ephesians 4:13-25 (NKJV)

13 till we all come to the unity of the faith and of the knowledge of the Son of God, to a perfect man, to the measure of the stature of the fullness of Christ; 14 that we should no longer be children, tossed to and fro and carried about with every wind of doctrine, by the trickery of men, in the cunning craftiness of deceitful plotting, 15 but, speaking the truth in love, may grow up in all things into Him who is the head—Christ— 16 from whom the whole body, joined and knit together by what every joint supplies, according to the effective working by which every part does its share, causes growth of the body for the edifying of itself in love.
The New Man
17 This I say, therefore, and testify in the Lord, that you should no longer walk as the rest of the Gentiles walk, in the futility of their mind, 18 having their understanding darkened, being alienated from the life of God, because of the ignorance that is in them, because of the blindness of their heart; 19 who, being past feeling, have given themselves over to lewdness, to work all uncleanness with greediness.
*20 But you have not so learned Christ, 21 **if indeed you have heard Him and have been taught by Him, as the truth is in Jesus: 22 that you put off, concerning your former conduct, the old man which grows corrupt according to the deceitful lusts,** 23 and be renewed in the spirit of your mind, 24 and that you put*

on the new man which was created according to God, in true righteousness and holiness.
Do Not Grieve the Spirit
25 Therefore, putting away lying, "Let each one of you speak truth with his neighbor," for we are members of one another.

Ephesians 4:13-25 amongst other items raised the fact that we need to shed off the old man or old sinful name and embrace the new man/woman that we have become from knowing and receiving Jesus Christ in our lives. "you put off, concerning the former conduct, the old man which grows corrupt according to the deceitful lusts". 'putting away lying, "let each of you speak truth with his neighbour," for we are members of one another'. We see the footprints of lying and deceitfulness carrying corruption with them everywhere they go. Only truth or the Spirit of Truth can set us free from corruption.

With these last paragraphs, we draw the curtain on the critical subject matter of lying, falsehoods and deceptions which are the original sin from the Garden of Eden. In the name of Jesus Christ and the power and authority He has given to Christiana and I, we rebuke back to hell every spirit or forces of lying, falsehoods, deceptions and corruption that wants to operate in your life or is already operating in your life right now. You must be born again for this prayer to mean anything to you and your situation. If you are not born again, please get born again in a rush before lying, falsehoods, deceptions and corruption impact your life in a way that you will not be able to recover from your losses.

Please use this prayer below to get born again if you cannot wait to get to a Church or fellowship. If you want to accept Jesus Christ for the first time or you want to rededicate your life to Jesus Christ, please read/say this Salvation prayer below:

Salvation Prayer

Jesus! I am a Sinner; I have Sinned against God and man. I cannot help myself. I believe you are the Son of God who came to this world to die for my Sins and for my sake. Please come into my life to save me from Sin and the devil. Please become my Lord and Saviour. Amen.

Congratulations! God bless you!

Bye! Ciao!

ABOUT THE AUTHORS

Ademola Usuanlele is a coordinator and Pastoring Disciple in Spirit and Life Family Bible Church and Godhead Prayer Ministry both in Edmonton, Alberta Canada. He is a New Man in Christ. He was an alternate cell group minister, an altar steward and an usher in Winners Chapel International in Edmonton, Alberta Canada. He is a former member of Gideon International. He enjoys Kingdom Advancement Prayers, singing, praising and serving Jesus Christ our Lord. He also enjoys traveling, working on complex projects, music, reading, and mentoring and learning new languages. More especially he enjoys spending time with his wife Christiana "Titilayo", daughter Pauline, son Ademola Jnr and his extended family. He is a past board director of Oliver Centre in Edmonton, Alberta and former board national treasurer and member Canadian Family Advisory Network (CFAN). He is the council former co-chair for the Edmonton, Alberta Canada Stollery Children's Hospital's Patient & Family-Centred Care Council (PFCCC). He is a former section Audit Chair of Edmonton Section of American Society for Quality (ASQ). He is the founder and board President of Ademola Usuanlele Charitable Foundation. Ademola Usuanlele is a former board director of both Canadian Council for Africa (CCAfrica) and Canada-Nigeria Chamber of Commerce. Ademola is the Chairman/CEO of Groupe Haus Incorporated, which is headquartered in Edmonton, Alberta, Canada and has subsidiaries in two African Countries.

Christiana Usuanlele is a Pastoring Disciple and virtuous woman who has been a devoted and a committed Christian and a church worker for many years. She was ordained a Pastor in Vineyard Christian Ministries in December 2000. She joined Spirit and Life Family Bible Church & Godhead Prayer Ministries in November 2014 where she hit the ground running with God's Kingdom Assignment. She is a Care Counsellor (Family Head for the New Member Zone) in Godhead International Christian Centre (GICC). She is the Assistant Secretary II at Spirit and Life Family Bible Church, Giwa-Amu in Benin City, Edo State, Nigeria. She is also on assignment to a local community Church in Edo Environs for Spirit and Life Family Bible Church. She is a very generous and cheerful giver. She enjoys praying, reading and teaching the Word of God. She also enjoys evangelism and members' follow-up. She is a sweet and devoted wife and mother.

ABOUT THE BOOK

Lying, falsehoods and deceptions are sin. They were the first combination of sin that devil delivered to Adam and Eve in the Garden of Eden which led to the fall of the first Adam and man. This eventually led to God sending Jesus Christ down in the form of human as the second Adam. Strangely, at the end of this world as we know it, lying, falsehoods and the deceptions of lucifer the devil will prevent very many from going to Heaven. This book was birthed by our book on Forgiveness. If you can get hold of the Forgiveness book before you read this book, it will ring a louder bell in your ears. You can read them in the order convenient to you. The pattern and structure of both books are identical. This book is a Kingdom Advancement Tool using various scriptures in the Bible and the Holy Spirit to portray lying, falsehoods and deceptions as a serious spiritual and physical issue that should be given all the attention it deserves. It explores some of the causes of lying and some of the spiritual and physical problems caused by lying. These problems caused include disunity, lack of prosperity, lack of peace, lack of everlasting joy, lack of love, stagnation of faith, stagnation of spiritual growth and a whole host of other problems. We have as led by the Spirit of God walked through some ways to stop lying, falsehoods and deceptions as directed by Jesus Christ and we have opened the door for those who want salvation and those who want to rededicate their lives to Jesus Christ. Please do not be shy about reading this book. If you truly believe that you do not have problems with lying, you can use the book to guide others to learn how to stop lying, falsehoods and deceptions or to prevent them from getting themselves entangled in lies/falsehoods and deception which is a Sin. Buy* and read a copy today! God bless you.

*A portion of the proceeds from the sale of this book will be given to Charities and Foundations. Such as Ademola Usuanlele Charitable Foundations worldwide, Sickle Cell Foundation of Alberta, Canadian Family Advisory Network, Canadian Premature Babies Foundation, Stollery Children's Hospital's Patient & Family Centred Care Council and Oliver Centre